THE BEST 50

BROWNIES AND BLONDIES

Mara Reid Rogers

Bristol Publishing Enterprises
San Leandro, California

Printed in the United States of America.

ISBN: 1-55867-255-9

Cover design: Frank J. Paredes
Cover photography: John A. Benson
Food stylist: Susan De Vaty

ABOUT BROWNIES AND BLONDIES

Brownies and blondies have long been an American favorite. Like the rest of us, you probably enjoy these scrumptious goodies with a passion. They're good for dessert, tucked into a lunchbox, slipped into a briefcase or as a snack any time of day. Brownies and blondies are even good for breakfast. Wrapped in a napkin, they make a perfect on-the-go morning meal; or enjoy them on your best china for brunch when guests are expected.

The recipes that follow, and many variations, will give you more than 50 choices at your fingertips. They will always bake perfectly if you follow the directions carefully. The valuable information that follows will make every batch a success.

POINTERS FOR MAKING BROWNIES AND BLONDIES

The Pan

- Brownies are easier to remove from nonstick pans, but cutting and removing them with metal knives and spatulas must be done carefully.
- Observe the baking pan sizes in recipes; otherwise the final results will be different in texture than intended by the recipe.
- If you are using a baking pan that is gray, glass, dull or dark (not with a shiny surface) and find that your brownies are overbaking at the oven temperature called for, reduce the oven temperature by 25°F.
- When greasing the pan before baking brownies, grease the bottom and sides of the pan, and make sure to grease the edges and corners also.
- After greasing the pan before baking brownies, use unsweetened cocoa powder to "flour" or "dust" the baking pan. This adds more flavor and prevents white residue on the exterior of the brownies from flour.
- Use vegetable shortening, nonstick vegetable spray or unsalted butter to grease baking pans, because salted butter tends to cause baked goods to stick to the pan. In addition it will cause over-browning at oven temperatures over 400°F.

The Measurements

· To get perfect brownies every time, it is important to use accurate measurements. Always use a glass or plastic calibrated measuring cup for liquids; metal or plastic calibrated measuring cups for dry ingredients; and standard measuring spoons.

· To read a liquid measuring cup accurately: Set the measuring cup down on your kitchen counter and pour in the contents to be measured. When the liquid settles, stoop down so that you are eye-level with the written measurements on the exterior of the measuring cup and read the measurement.

· Measure flour by spooning it (do not pack it) into metal or plastic dry measuring cups and leveling the top with a knife or small spatula. The same rule applies to using measuring spoons; spoon the ingredient using the measuring spoon and level the top using a knife. If the recipe calls for a "heaping" specific measurement, do not level the contents.

- In altitudes up to 3,500 feet, for brownies rich in chocolate or nuts, a reduction of about one-half the baking powder or baking soda may be advisable. At very high altitudes, a slight reduction in sugar may help, but in general, the baking soda should not be reduced beyond $\frac{1}{2}$ teaspoon for each cup of milk or cream used. However, the best way to discover exact quantities for each recipe change is by experimenting.

Ingredients
- Unless otherwise instructed, all ingredients normally stored in the refrigerator, such as eggs, cream cheese, butter, and milk, should be used at room temperature. Remove them from the refrigerator 30 minutes before using.
- Always use unsalted butter whenever butter is called for.
- "Softened butter" means butter that is just that — softened, not runny. Softened butter has been removed from the refrigerator about 30 minutes before using.
- Some recipes call for "lightly beaten" eggs, because they are more easily incorporated into the other ingredients.
- Cool melted butter before adding to mixture. For example, if you add flour to a hot mixture, it will gelatinize, and the brownies will be heavy and eraser-like.

- Spray the pan used to melt chocolate with nonstick vegetable spray and the chocolate will slip right out.
- Chocolate should be melted slowly over very low heat, since it scorches quickly. The same rule applies to white chocolate (not truly "chocolate" since it doesn't contain chocolate liquor). The easiest and most foolproof melting method is to place coarsely chopped (to ensure even melting) chocolate in the top of a double boiler over hot, barely simmering water. Stir the chocolate constantly until the chocolate is soft and shiny — a little more than halfway melted. Immediately remove the top pan from the heat and continue stirring the chocolate until it is completely melted, smooth and still shiny.
- To melt chocolate in a microwave oven: Place the chocolate in a microwave-safe bowl (a microwave-safe glass measuring cup with handle works well) and heat at MEDIUM (50 percent power), until almost melted, stirring every 30 seconds. Remove from the microwave oven and stir the chocolate until completely melted, smooth and still shiny. Four ounces of chocolate will take about 3 minutes in a 650- to 700-watt oven. However, the timing will vary depending on the oven and the type and amount of chocolate. For example, white chocolate tends to scorch very quickly, so it should be watched carefully.

- Whichever method you use to melt chocolate or any flavor of morsels or chips (such as peanut butter or butterscotch), since it scorches quickly, never take your eyes off it while it is melting.
- Note that chocolate chips (or flavored morsels or chips) melt faster than squares. Various chocolates have different consistencies when melted. Unsweetened chocolate becomes runny; semisweet, sweet and white chocolates hold their shape until stirred (so don't wait for them to "look" melted or you are liable to burn them).
- Although chocolate can be melted with liquid, even a single bead of liquid dropped into melted chocolate will cause it to "seize" (clump and harden). Though seizing can sometimes be corrected, it is recommend that you start over entirely.
- Cool melted chocolate to room temperature before adding to brownie batters. Otherwise, you are liable to melt the fat in the batter, which will cause a textural change in the final baked product.
- Use regular, not low-fat, sour cream and cream cheese to produce the best results.
- Don't overmix brownie batter; overmixing makes brownies tough.

The Oven
- For even baking, position the rack in the center of the oven, and bake brownies in the center of the rack. If your oven bakes unevenly, turn the pan halfway through the baking time.
- You can purchase an oven thermometer to see if your true oven temperature is what the oven dial reads. For example, if you set the oven dial at 350° F, but after 10 minutes of preheating your oven, the oven thermometer reads 325°F, your oven is baking 25° cooler than the actual oven dial reading. You must make an adjustment and increase the baking temperature called for in the recipe by 25°.
- To avoid overbaked, dry brownies, always check brownies for doneness 10 minutes before the end of the baking time, as bakeware material can affect how quickly the brownies bake. A perfectly baked batch of brownies should have a thin, crackled crust and slightly risen edge.

Cutting and Storage
- For easier cutting, and to prevent irregular edges, use a serrated knife to score the brownies as soon as the pan comes out of the oven. Then cut the cooled bars along the scored lines.

- The best way to store these goodies so they do not dry out is, once the cooled brownies have been cut into squares, layer them in an airtight tin (such as a metal cookie tin), separating layers with sheets of waxed paper. Or, individually wrap the brownies in plastic wrap or waxed paper and stack them in the tin. If iced, frosted or glazed, lightly spray the paper or wrap with nonstick vegetable spray before wrapping to prevent waxed paper or plastic wrap from sticking to the topping.
- Some recipes will direct you to store the brownies in the refrigerator; for example, all brownies made with sour cream or cream cheese should be refrigerated in an airtight tin.
- Though it is rare that brownies are not eaten within a couple of days after baking, they freeze well. To prepare them for freezing: Remove the entire layer of brownies from the pan once cooled (do not score or cut them) and wrap in sheets of plastic wrap. Store in a thick, sturdy, self-sealing plastic bag designed for the freezer, or in a sturdy, freezer-safe storage container with a lid that closes tightly. Label with an indelible marker with the recipe name, quantity and date. Defrost overnight in the refrigerator until completely thawed, then unwrap, score and cut into separate bars.

SPECIAL TOUCHES

Want more decadence to round out the luscious recipes in this book? Besides brownies à la mode (crowned with a scoop of your favorite ice cream or sorbet), here are some speedy topping ideas for your "from scratch" brownies or blondies or to gussy up your favorite batch of brownies or blondies from a packaged mix.

Just Before Serving

- Drizzle brownies with chocolate syrup.
- Spread brownies with a commercially prepared ice cream topping such as pineapple, butterscotch or marshmallow.
- For Christmas brownies: Decorate each brownie to resemble Santa Claus. Cut out cooled brownies with a round cookie-cutter (save any scraps for another day, as a topping, or to mix with ice cream.) Spread each round brownie evenly with commercially prepared white vanilla. For hat, sprinkle top third and halfway down one side of the brownie with red sugar (available at supermarket). Place mini candy coated chocolate pieces on frosting for eyes and nose (use 2 green M & M's® for eyes, and one red M & M® for nose.) Cut mini marshmallows in half lengthwise, place at edge of red sugar for hat brim. Use mini marshmallows for hat tassel and beard.

- Sprinkle frosted bars with any candy, such as chocolate-dipped espresso beans, crushed hard peppermint candy, crushed toffee, crushed chocolate malt balls, chocolate-covered candied orange peel or chocolate-covered candied ginger strips.
- Top brownies or blondies with the myriad flavors of whipped toppings available now at your supermarket.
- Adorn them with one of the many pie toppings now available such as apple, blueberry, cherry, or even huckleberry.
- Try one of many canned frostings from vanilla to coconut-pecan.
- Make homemade whipped cream and lace it with your favorite liqueur just before topping brownies or blondies.
- With a serrated knife, split a brownie in half horizontally and fill with your favorite ice cream for an ice cream sandwich made better.

JUST BEFORE BAKING

- With a table knife, swirl orange marmalade, ginger preserves, lemon curd or seedless jam through brownie batter with a gentle back and forth motion to create a marbled effect.

- Garnish with nuts, toasted or not. Try macadamia nuts (don't toast them), pecans, walnuts, almonds, hazelnuts, cashews or peanuts. Toasting nuts enhances their flavor. To toast nuts, heat oven to 350°F. Spread the nuts, with papery skins removed, evenly in a pie plate or shallow baking dish and bake for 5 to 8 minutes or until golden brown and fragrant, stirring occasionally.

- Scatter brownies with dried banana chips or chopped dried fruit such as dried tart cherries, dates or dried peaches.

- Garnish with toasted coconut. To toast sweetened, flaked coconut: Spread coconut in a single layer on a baking sheet with shallow sides. Bake for 5 to 8 minutes in a 325°F oven, tossing often, or until toasted light golden brown.

- Garnish with a trio of chips or morsels: peanut butter, butterscotch and chocolate.

SUPREME FUDGY BROWNIES

Just before serving, spread these brownies with marshmallow ice cream topping for a double delight.

2 tsp. butter

1 tbs. unsweetened cocoa powder

1 cup butter, melted and cooled

2 oz. unsweetened chocolate, melted and cooled (see page 5)

5 oz. bittersweet chocolate, melted and cooled

$^2/_3$ cup unbleached all-purpose flour

$^1/_2$ tsp. salt

1 cup granulated sugar

2 large eggs, lightly beaten

1 large egg yolk, lightly beaten

2 tsp. pure vanilla extract

Heat oven to 350°F. Grease an 8-inch square baking pan with 2 tsp. butter. Dust with cocoa powder; invert pan and tap to release excess.

Whisk melted butter and chocolates together in a large bowl. Whisk in flour, salt and sugar. Whisk in eggs, egg yolk and vanilla until well blended.

Pour batter into baking pan. Bake in center of oven for 25 to 35 minutes, or until a toothpick inserted in the center comes out with a few moist crumbs, but not wet batter. Cool thoroughly in pan on a wire rack, about 1 hour.

Cut into 16 (2-inch) square bars and remove from pan. Makes 16.

ALMOND-CHEESECAKE BROWNIES

For lemon-cheesecake brownies substitute lemon extract for the almond extract and 1 tsp. lemon zest for sliced almond garnish. Sprinkle with the lemon zest just after brownies come from the oven.

BROWNIES

2 tsp. unsalted butter
1 tbs. unsweetened cocoa powder
5 oz. bittersweet chocolate,
  melted and cooled (see page 5)
6 tbs. butter, melted and cooled

3/4 cup granulated sugar
1/4 cup unbleached all-purpose flour
1/4 tsp. baking powder
1/4 tsp. salt

CHEESECAKE

8 oz. cream cheese, softened
1/2 cup granulated sugar
2 tbs. unbleached all-purpose

flour
3/4 tsp. almond extract
2 large eggs

TOPPING

1 1/2 cups sour cream
1/2 cup confectioners' sugar, sifted

1/2 tsp. pure vanilla extract
2/3 cup sliced almonds for garnish

Heat oven to 350°F. Grease an 8-inch square baking pan with 2 tsp. butter. Dust with cocoa powder; invert pan and tap to release excess.

Stir together melted chocolate and butter in a medium bowl until well blended. Stir in sugar, flour, baking powder and salt until well blended and smooth. Spread batter evenly in pan.

Prepare cheesecake: With an electric mixer, beat cream cheese, sugar, flour and almond extract in a medium bowl on medium speed until light and fluffy, about 2 minutes. Add eggs, one at a time, beating after each addition, just until well blended and smooth.

Spread cheesecake mixture evenly over brownies. Bake on center oven rack for 20 minutes, or until cheesecake layer is almost set.

While brownies bake, prepare topping: Stir sour cream, confectioners' sugar and vanilla in a small bowl until well blended. Cover and refrigerate.

Remove pan from oven and pour sour cream mixture over brownies, smoothing surface. Sprinkle evenly with almonds. Return pan to oven and bake for 15 to 20 minutes, or until topping is set and puffs up, and almonds are light brown. Cool thoroughly in pan on a wire rack, about 1 hour.

Cut into 16 (2-inch) square bars and remove from pan. Store in the refrigerator. Makes 16.

FUDGY CARAMEL BROWNIES

For infinite variations, after drizzling the brownies with the caramel ice cream topping, sprinkle them with your choice of candy.

2 tsp. butter
1 tbs. unsweetened cocoa powder
3/4 cup light brown sugar, packed
3/4 cup granulated sugar
4 large eggs
3/4 cup unbleached all-purpose flour
1/4 tsp. salt
6 oz. bittersweet chocolate, melted and cooled (see page 5)
1 cup butter, melted and cooled
1 tsp. pure vanilla extract
1 jar (12 oz.) caramel topping

Heat oven to 350°F. Grease an 8-inch square baking pan with 2 tsp. butter. Dust with cocoa powder; invert pan and tap to release excess.

With an electric mixer, beat sugars and eggs on high speed in a large bowl until light in color and thickened, about 3 minutes. Sift flour and salt on a sheet of waxed paper and add to bowl with melted chocolate, butter and vanilla. With a rubber spatula, stir gently just until well blended. Spread batter evenly in pan.

Bake in center of oven for 25 to 30 minutes, or until brownies begin to pull away from the sides of pan. Cool thoroughly in pan on a wire rack, about 1 hour.

Cut into 16 (2-x-3-inch) rectangular bars and remove from pan. Serve drizzled with caramel topping. Makes 16.

ROCKY ROADS

These brownies remind you of the popular ice cream of the same name. You can substitute any type of nut for the walnuts and still call them **Rocky Roads**.

2 tsp. butter
1 tbs. unsweetened cocoa powder
1/2 cup semisweet chocolate chips
1 cup miniature marshmallows
1/2 cup coarsely chopped walnuts
2 tbs. unbleached all-purpose flour
1/2 cup butter, melted and cooled
2 oz. unsweetened chocolate, melted and cooled (see page 5)
3/4 cup unbleached all-purpose flour
1 tbs. unsweetened cocoa powder
3/4 cup granulated sugar
1/4 tsp. salt
2 large eggs, lightly beaten
1 tsp. pure vanilla extract

Heat oven to 350°F. Grease an 8-inch square baking pan with 2 tsp. butter. Dust with cocoa powder; invert pan and tap to release excess.

Combine chocolate chips, marshmallows and walnuts with 2 tbs. flour in a small bowl until coated. Set aside.

With a fork, vigorously stir melted butter and chocolate together in a large bowl. Blend in flour, cocoa, sugar and salt. Stir in eggs and vanilla extract until well blended. Stir in chocolate chip-marshmallow-walnut mixture until blended. Spread batter evenly in pan.

Bake in center of oven for 25 to 30 minutes, or until a toothpick inserted in the center comes out with a few moist crumbs, but not wet batter. Cool thoroughly in pan on a wire rack, about 1 hour.

Cut into 16 (2-inch) square bars and remove from pan. Makes 16.

MARBLED BROWNIES

Marbled brownies are not only irresistible, they are one of the prettiest brownies around.

CREAM CHEESE LAYER

1/4 cup granulated sugar
8 oz. cream cheese, softened

1 large egg yolk, lightly beaten
1/2 tsp. pure vanilla extract

BROWNIES

2 tsp. butter
1 tbs. unsweetened cocoa powder
1 cup butter, melted and cooled
3 oz. unsweetened chocolate,
   melted and cooled (see page 5)
4 oz. bittersweet chocolate,
   melted and cooled

2/3 cup unbleached all-purpose flour
1/2 tsp. salt
1 cup granulated sugar
2 large eggs, lightly beaten
1 large egg yolk, lightly beaten
2 tsp. pure vanilla extract

Combine cream cheese layer ingredients in a small bowl and stir vigorously with a fork until well blended. Cover and refrigerate until ready to use.

Heat oven to 350°F. Grease an 8-inch square baking pan with 2 tsp. butter. Dust with cocoa powder; invert pan and tap to release excess.

Whisk melted butter and melted chocolates together in a large bowl. Whisk in flour, salt and sugar. Whisk in eggs, egg yolk and vanilla until well blended. Pour ³⁄₄ of the brownie batter into pan. With a fork, reblend cream-cheese mixture if necessary, and spread evenly over brownie batter. Top with remaining brownie batter in an even layer.

Starting at one corner of pan, insert a table knife halfway down into batter and cream-cheese layers, but not to bottom of pan. Draw knife back and forth in a gentle, swirling motion from one side of pan to the opposite side, down length of the pan, to create a marbled effect.

Bake in center of oven for 40 to 50 minutes, or until a toothpick inserted in the center comes out with a few moist crumbs, but not wet batter. Cool thoroughly in pan on a wire rack, about 1 hour.

Cut into 16 (2-inch) square bars and remove from pan. Store in the refrigerator. Makes 16.

RASPBERRY TRUFFLE BROWNIES

Substitute any other jam flavor and sorbet to serve, and you'll instantly be able to create a rainbow of different truffle brownies. Try strawberry to begin with...

2 tsp. butter
1 tbs. unsweetened cocoa powder
1 cup butter, melted and cooled
3 oz. semisweet chocolate, melted and cooled (see page 5)
4 oz. bittersweet chocolate, melted and cooled
2/3 cup unbleached all-purpose flour
1/2 tsp. salt
1 cup granulated sugar
2 large eggs, lightly beaten
1 large egg yolk, lightly beaten
2 tsp. pure vanilla extract
1 cup seedless red raspberry jam, divided
raspberry sorbet

Heat oven to 350°F. Grease an 8-inch square baking pan with 2 tsp. butter. Dust with cocoa powder; invert pan and tap to release excess.

Whisk melted butter and melted chocolates together in a large bowl until well blended. Whisk in flour, salt and sugar until well blended. Whisk in lightly beaten eggs, egg yolk and vanilla until well blended. Spread ³/₄ of the batter evenly in pan. With a ¹/₄ tsp. measuring spoon, spoon half of the raspberry jam evenly over batter (jam will cover much, but not all, of brownie layer). Pour remaining brownie batter over all and spread evenly, gently pressing down.

Bake in center of oven for 50 to 60 minutes, or until surface is set and a toothpick inserted in the center comes out with a few moist crumbs, but not wet batter. Cool thoroughly in pan on a wire rack, about 1 hour.

Cut into 16 (2-inch) square bars and remove from pan. Serve each brownie topped with a scoop of raspberry sorbet (brownies à la mode). Store uneaten brownies in the refrigerator. Makes 16.

THE ULTIMATE DOUBLE-CHOCOLATE BROWNIES

You can transform these into "triple-chocolate" by frosting them with a bittersweet chocolate frosting.

2 tsp. butter
1 tbs. unsweetened cocoa powder
1 1/4 cups unbleached all-purpose flour
3/4 tsp. baking powder
1/4 tsp. salt
3/4 cup butter, softened
3 tbs. vegetable shortening
1 cup granulated sugar
3 large eggs, lightly beaten
2 large egg yolks, lightly beaten
2 tbs. vegetable oil
4 oz. semisweet chocolate, melted and cooled (see page 5)
2 oz. unsweetened chocolate, melted and cooled
2 tsp. pure vanilla extract

Heat oven to 350°F. Grease an 8-inch square baking pan with 2 tsp. butter. Dust with cocoa powder; invert pan and tap to release excess.

Sift together flour, baking powder and salt onto a sheet of waxed paper and set aside. With an electric mixer, beat butter and vegetable shortening on medium speed in a large bowl for 2 minutes, or until well blended. Gradually pour in sugar and continue to beat until mixture is light and fluffy, about 2 minutes.

Add eggs, egg yolks and vegetable oil; beat on medium speed until mixture is well blended. On low speed, beat in melted chocolates and vanilla. Add dry mixture and beat on medium speed until no white streaks are visible, about 30 seconds. (Do not overbeat.) Spread batter evenly in pan.

Bake in center of oven for 30 to 35 minutes or until a toothpick inserted in the center comes out clean with a few moist crumbs, but not wet batter. Cool thoroughly in the pan on a wire rack, about 1 hour.

Cut into 16 (2-inch) square bars and remove from pan. Makes 16.

CAPPUCCINO BROWNIES

Chocolate-covered espresso beans are available at gourmet shops, candy stores and coffee shops.

2 tsp. butter
1 tbs. unsweetened cocoa powder
1 1/4 cups unbleached all-purpose
  flour
3/4 tsp. baking powder
1/4 tsp. salt
3/4 cup butter, softened
3 tbs. vegetable shortening
1 cup granulated sugar
3 large eggs, lightly beaten

2 large egg yolks, lightly beaten
2 tbs. vegetable oil
4 oz. semisweet chocolate, melted
  and cooled (see page 5)
2 oz. unsweetened chocolate,
  melted and cooled
2 tsp. pure vanilla extract
2 tbs. instant espresso coffee
  granules

TOPPING

1 cup sour cream
2/3 cup confectioners' sugar
8 oz. cream cheese

1/2 tsp. ground cinnamon
1/3 cup chocolate-covered espresso
  beans for garnish

Heat oven to 350°F. Grease an 8-inch square baking pan with 2 tsp. butter. Dust with cocoa powder; invert pan and tap to release excess.

Sift together flour, baking powder and salt onto a sheet of waxed paper and set aside. With an electric mixer, beat butter and shortening on medium speed in a large bowl for 2 minutes or until well blended. Gradually pour in sugar, and beat until mixture is light and fluffy, about 2 minutes.

Add eggs, egg yolks and vegetable oil; beat on medium speed until well blended. On low speed, beat in melted chocolates, vanilla and instant coffee until well blended. Add dry mixture and beat on medium speed until no white streaks are visible, about 30 seconds. (Do not over-beat.) Spread batter evenly in pan.

Bake in center of oven for 30 to 35 minutes or until a toothpick inserted in the center comes out clean with a few moist crumbs, but not wet batter. Cool thoroughly in the pan on a wire rack, about 1 hour.

Prepare topping: With an electric mixer, beat sour cream, confectioners' sugar, cream cheese and cinnamon on medium-high speed in a medium bowl until well blended, about 2 minutes. Spread topping evenly over brownies and scatter with chocolate-covered espresso beans.

Cut into 16 (2-inch) square bars and remove from pan. Store in the refrigerator. Makes 16.

MINT MELTAWAYS

After frosting, sprinkle these with crushed hard peppermint candy.

FROSTING

1¾ cups confectioners' sugar,
  sifted
½ cup butter, softened

2 tbs. heavy whipping cream
1 tsp. peppermint extract
1-2 drops green food coloring

BROWNIES

2 tsp. butter
1 tbs. unsweetened cocoa powder
1¼ cups unbleached all-purpose
  flour
¾ tsp. baking powder
¼ tsp. salt
¾ cup butter, softened
3 tbs. vegetable shortening
1 cup granulated sugar

3 large eggs, lightly beaten
2 large egg yolks, lightly beaten
2 tbs. vegetable oil
4 oz. semisweet chocolate, melted
  and cooled (see page 5)
2 oz. unsweetened chocolate,
  melted and cooled
2 tsp. peppermint extract

To prepare frosting: In a large electric mixer bowl, beat confectioners' sugar, butter and cream on medium-high speed until well blended, about 30 seconds. Do not overbeat. Add peppermint and food coloring and beat 5 seconds more just until blended. Cover and refrigerate until ready to use.

Heat oven to 350°F. Grease an 8-inch square baking pan with 2 tsp. butter. Dust with cocoa powder; invert pan and tap to release excess.

Sift together flour, baking powder and salt onto a sheet of waxed paper. With an electric mixer, beat butter and shortening on medium speed in a large bowl for 2 minutes, or until well blended. Gradually pour in sugar and beat until mixture is light and fluffy, about 2 minutes.

Add eggs, egg yolks and vegetable oil; beat on medium speed until mixture is well blended. On low speed, beat in melted chocolates and peppermint extract until well blended. Add dry mixture and beat on medium until no white streaks are visible, about 30 seconds. (Do not overbeat.) Spread batter evenly in pan.

Bake in center of oven for 30 to 35 minutes or until a toothpick inserted in the center comes out clean with a few moist crumbs, but not wet batter. Cool thoroughly in pan on a wire rack, about 1 hour.

Run a paring knife around inside edge of pan. Invert brownies onto a serving plate and invert them again so crust is on top. Just before serving, spread frosting evenly over brownies. Cut into 16 (2-inch) square bars and serve at once. Store any remaining brownies in the refrigerator. Makes 16.

CHOCOLATE-SOUR CREAM FROSTED BROWNIES

This is the most "adult" of the brownies in this book. Kids don't like the sophisticated chocolate sour cream frosting as much as adults do.

FROSTING

5 oz. semisweet chocolate, melted and cooled (see page 5)
2/3 cup sour cream

BROWNIES

2 tsp. butter
1 tbs. unsweetened cocoa powder
1 1/4 cups unbleached all-purpose
  flour
3/4 tsp. baking powder
1/4 tsp. salt
3/4 cup butter, softened
3 tbs. vegetable shortening
1 cup granulated sugar

3 large eggs, lightly beaten
2 large egg yolks, lightly beaten
2 tbs. vegetable oil
4 oz. semisweet chocolate, melted
  and cooled (see page 5)
2 oz. unsweetened chocolate,
  melted and cooled
2 tsp. pure vanilla extract

Prepare frosting: In a medium bowl, stir together melted chocolate and sour cream until well blended. Cover and refrigerate until ready to use.

Heat oven to 350°F. Grease an 8-inch square baking pan with 2 tsp. butter. Dust with cocoa powder; invert pan and tap to release excess.

Sift together flour, baking powder and salt onto a sheet of waxed paper and set aside. With an electric mixer, beat butter and shortening on medium speed in a large bowl for 2 minutes, or until well blended. Gradually pour in sugar and beat until mixture is light and fluffy, about 2 minutes. Add eggs, egg yolks and vegetable oil; beat on medium speed until mixture is well blended. On low speed, beat in melted chocolates and vanilla. Add dry mixture and beat on medium until no white streaks are visible, about 30 seconds. (Do not overbeat.) Spread batter evenly in pan.

Bake in center of oven for 30 to 35 minutes or until a toothpick inserted in the center comes out clean with a few moist crumbs, but not wet batter. Cool thoroughly in pan on a wire rack, about 1 hour.

Spread frosting evenly over brownies. Cut into 16 (2-inch) square bars and remove from pan. Store in the refrigerator. Makes 16.

BROWNIES WITH MAPLE-PECAN GLAZE

This glaze is delicious served over ice cream, too.

2 tsp. butter
1 tbs. unsweetened cocoa powder
1 1/4 cups unbleached all-purpose
   flour
3/4 tsp. baking powder
1/4 tsp. salt
3/4 cup butter, softened
3 tbs. vegetable shortening
1 cup granulated sugar

3 large eggs, lightly beaten
2 large egg yolks, lightly beaten
2 tbs. vegetable oil
4 oz. semisweet chocolate, melted
   and cooled (see page 5)
2 oz. unsweetened chocolate,
   melted and cooled
2 tsp. pure vanilla extract

GLAZE

2 oz. pecan halves
1 1/4 cups confectioners' sugar
1/4 cup butter, softened
1/8 cup unsweetened cocoa powder

1/8 cup heavy whipping cream,
   room temperature
1/8 tsp. freshly ground black pepper
2 tsp. maple extract

Heat oven to 350°F. Grease an 8-inch square baking pan with 2 tsp.

butter. Dust with cocoa powder; invert pan and tap to release excess.

Sift together flour, baking powder and salt onto a sheet of waxed paper and set aside. With an electric mixer, beat butter and shortening on medium speed in a large bowl for 2 minutes, or until well blended. Gradually pour in sugar and beat until mixture is light and fluffy, about 2 minutes.

Add eggs, egg yolks and vegetable oil and beat on medium speed until well blended. On low speed, beat in melted chocolates and vanilla. Add dry mixture and beat on medium until no white streaks are visible, about 30 seconds. (Do not overbeat.) Spread batter evenly in pan.

Bake in center of oven for 30 to 35 minutes or until a toothpick inserted in the center comes out clean with a few moist crumbs, but not wet batter. Do not turn oven off. Cool thoroughly in pan on a wire rack, about 1 hour.

Prepare glaze: Bake pecan halves in one layer on a baking sheet for 4 to 6 minutes, or until lightly toasted and fragrant; do not overcook. Cool to room temperature, chop coarsely, transfer to a medium bowl with confectioners' sugar and set aside.

Combine butter, cocoa powder and cream in a heavy 1-quart saucepan over medium-high heat. Stir frequently until butter is melted and mixture is smooth. Bring just to a boil, about 1 minute. Immediately pour into bowl with pecan mixture; add pepper and maple extract and stir until well blended. Spread glaze evenly over brownies. Refrigerate for 15 minutes or just until surface of glaze hardens. Cut into 16 square bars and remove from pan.

SENSATIONALLY CHEWY BROWNIES

Turn to Special Touches, *pages 9–11, for a multitude of variations.*

2 tsp. butter
1 tbs. unsweetened cocoa powder
1 1/4 cups unbleached all-purpose flour
2/3 cup unsweetened cocoa powder
1/4 tsp. baking soda
3/4 tsp. salt
2 cups granulated sugar
2/3 cup vegetable oil
1/4 cup water
1/4 cup whole milk
1 large egg
1 large egg yolk
2 tsp. pure vanilla extract

Heat oven to 350°F. Grease an 8-inch square baking pan with 2 tsp. butter. Dust with cocoa powder; invert pan and tap to release excess.

Sift flour, $\frac{2}{3}$ cup cocoa powder, baking soda, salt and sugar into a large bowl. Add oil, water, milk, egg, egg yolk and vanilla extract. Stir vigorously with a fork until mixture is well blended. Spread batter evenly in pan.

Bake in center of oven for 25 to 35 minutes or until a toothpick inserted in the center comes out clean, with a few moist crumbs, but not wet batter. Cool thoroughly in pan on a wire rack, about 1 hour.

Cut into 16 (2-inch) square bars and remove from pan. Makes 16.

CHOCOLATE-PIÑA COLADA BROWNIES

You will need to make the topping for these unique brownies at least 4 hours before serving.

TOPPING

1 can (10 oz) frozen piña colada
    mix concentrate, thawed
6 large egg yolks, lightly beaten
1½ cups half-and-half, room
    temperature

¼ cup cornstarch
3 tbs. butter
½ cup sweetened, flaked coconut
1 tsp. coconut extract or pure
    vanilla extract

BROWNIES

2 tsp. butter
1 tbs. unsweetened cocoa powder
6 tbs. butter, melted and cooled
6 oz. semisweet chocolate, melted
    and cooled (see page 5)
¾ cup unbleached all-purpose flour

½ tsp. baking powder
¼ tsp. salt
¾ light brown sugar, packed
2 large eggs, lightly beaten
2 tsp. pure vanilla extract

½ cup sweetened, flaked coconut, toasted (see page 11)

Prepare topping: Bring piña colada concentrate, egg yolks, half-and-half and cornstarch to a boil in a 3- to 4-quart saucepan over medium heat, whisking constantly. Boil for 1 minute, whisking constantly until well blended, smooth and very thick.

Remove from heat at once and whisk in butter, $\frac{1}{2}$ cup coconut and coconut extract until well blended and butter has melted. Pour mixture into a heatproof bowl and cool to room temperature. Cover and refrigerate for at least 4 hours or until ready to use.

Heat oven to 350°F. Grease a 9-x-13-inch baking pan with 2 tsp. butter. Dust with cocoa powder; invert pan and tap to release excess.

Prepare brownies: Stir together melted butter and melted chocolate in a large bowl. Stir in remaining brownie ingredients until well blended. Spread batter evenly in pan.

Bake for 20 to 25 minutes or until a toothpick inserted in the center comes out clean, with a few moist crumbs, but not wet batter. Cool thoroughly in pan on a wire rack, about 1 hour.

Run a paring knife around inside edge of pan. Spread topping on top of brownies and sprinkle evenly with $\frac{1}{2}$ cup toasted coconut. Cut into 16 (2-by-3-inch) rectangular bars and remove from pan. Store in the refrigerator. Makes 16.

CHEWY MACAROON BROWNIES

Vary these brownies by pressing whole almonds into the macaroon surface just before serving.

2 tsp. butter

MACAROON LAYER

2²/₃ cups sweetened flaked
    coconut
¹/₂ cup plus 2 tbs. sweetened
    condensed milk

¹/₂ tsp. almond extract
1 large egg, lightly beaten

BROWNIE LAYER

6 tbs. butter, melted and cooled
6 oz. semisweet chocolate, melted
    and cooled (see page 5)
³/₄ cup unbleached all-purpose
    flour

¹/₂ tsp. baking powder
¹/₄ tsp. salt
³/₄ cup dark brown sugar, packed
2 large eggs, lightly beaten
2 tsp. pure vanilla extract

Heat oven to 350°F. Grease a 9-x-13-inch baking pan with 2 tsp. butter. Line pan with aluminum foil to cover pan bottom and 1/2-inch up sides.

Prepare macaroon layer: Stir together all ingredients for macaroon layer until well blended. Spread in evenly in pan. Bake in center of oven for 10 minutes.

Prepare brownie layer: Stir together melted butter and melted chocolate in a large bowl. Stir in remaining brownie layer ingredients until well blended.

After coconut mixture has baked for 10 minutes, remove pan from oven. Working quickly with a wooden spoon, gently spread brownie batter over coconut layer evenly; smooth top.

Immediately return pan to oven and bake for 20 to 30 minutes or until the surface is uniformly colored with no indentations, and a toothpick inserted in the center comes out clean, with a few moist crumbs, but not wet batter. Cool in pan on a wire rack for 30 minutes; brownies will not be thoroughly cool. Run a paring knife around inside edge of pan and invert pan to remove brownies. Carefully peel off foil in small pieces.

Dip knife into hot water between cuts, since macaroon tends to stick. Cut into 16 (2-by-3-inch) rectangular bars and remove from pan, inverting brownies so macaroon layer is on top. Makes 16.

LEMON BARS WITH BLACK BOTTOM CRUST

Your supermarket carries packaged Oreo® chocolate cookie crumbs.

2 tsp. butter

CRUST

1 cup Oreo® chocolate cookie crumbs or Famous™ chocolate wafer crumbs (16 wafers)

3 tbs. granulated sugar
1/4 cup butter, melted

FILLING

2 cups granulated sugar
1/4 cup unbleached all-purpose flour
1 tsp. baking powder
1/3 cup fresh lemon juice

1 tbs. freshly grated lemon zest
4 large eggs, lightly beaten
1/2 tsp. pure lemon extract

GLAZE

2 cups confectioners' sugar
2-4 tbs. whole milk

3/4 tsp. pure lemon extract

Heat oven to 350°F. Grease an 8-inch square baking pan with 2 tsp. butter.

Prepare crust: In a small bowl, mix together all crust ingredients until well blended. With the back of a large spoon, press crust mixture firmly in an even layer on bottom, corners and 1/4-inch up sides of pan. Bake crust in center of oven for 8 to 10 minutes, or just until firm to the touch.

Working quickly, make filling: Sift granulated sugar, flour and baking powder into a large bowl. Whisk in lemon juice and lemon zest until well blended. Whisk in eggs and lemon extract until well blended. Pour mixture into hot crust and immediately return to oven. Bake for 40 to 50 minutes or until surface is set. Cool thoroughly in pan on a wire rack, about 1 hour.

Prepare glaze: Place confectioners' sugar in a small bowl, add 2 tbs. of the milk and stir until well blended. Add milk, 1/2 tablespoon at a time as needed, while stirring, until glaze is just thin enough to pour, but not too runny. Stir in lemon extract until well blended. Spread glaze evenly over cool Lemon Bars. Refrigerate for 15 minutes, or until glaze surface hardens just enough so bars can be cut without leaving a jagged edge.

Cut into 16 (2-inch) square bars and remove from pan. Store in the refrigerator. Makes 16.

BROWNIES WITH CHEESECAKE FROSTING

You can vary this recipe by trying some of the other cream cheese flavors on the market.

2 tsp. butter
1 tbs. unsweetened cocoa powder
1 1/4 cups unbleached all-purpose
  flour
2/3 cup unsweetened cocoa powder
1/4 tsp. baking soda
3/4 tsp. salt

2 cups granulated sugar
2/3 cup vegetable oil
1/4 cup water
1/4 cup whole milk
1 large egg
1 large egg yolk
2 tsp. pure vanilla extract

FROSTING

2 containers (8 oz. each) Kraft® Philadelphia Flavors™
  Cheesecake Flavor Cream Cheese Spread
1 cup confectioners' sugar

Heat oven to 350°F. Grease a 9-x-13-inch baking pan with 2 tsp. butter. Dust with cocoa powder; invert pan and tap to release excess.

Sift flour, 2/3 cup cocoa powder, baking soda, salt and sugar into a large bowl. Add vegetable oil, water, milk, egg, egg yolk and vanilla extract. Stir vigorously with a fork until well blended. Spread batter evenly in pan.

Bake in center of oven for 25 to 35 minutes or until surface is uniformly colored with no indentations, and a toothpick inserted in the center comes out clean, with a few moist crumbs, but not wet batter. Cool thoroughly in pan on a wire rack, about 1 hour.

Prepare frosting: Combine Cheesecake Flavor Cream Cheese Spread and confectioners' sugar together in a large bowl. With a fork, vigorously stir until well blended and smooth. Spread frosting over brownies. Cut into 16 (2-x-3-inch) rectangular bars and remove from pan. Store in the refrigerator. Makes 16.

TWO-TONED MILK CHOCOLATE-PECAN BROWNIES

It's no secret that milk chocolate and peanuts go well together — so try coarsely chopped peanuts (not toasted) in place of the pecans.

2 tsp. butter
1 tbs. unbleached all-purpose flour
1 cup butter
2 cups light brown sugar, packed
2 cups unbleached all-purpose flour
1 tsp. baking powder
$\frac{1}{2}$ tsp. salt
2 large eggs, lightly beaten
2 tsp. vanilla extract
1 cup coarsely chopped pecans, toasted (see page 11)
1 pkg. (11$\frac{1}{2}$ oz.) milk chocolate chips
1 can (14 oz.) sweetened condensed milk
1 tbs. butter

Heat oven to 350°F. Grease a 9-x-13-inch baking pan with 2 tsp. butter. Dust with cocoa powder; invert pan and tap to release excess.

With an electric mixer, beat 1 cup butter and brown sugar on medium speed until light and fluffy, about 1 minute. Beat in flour, baking powder and salt on medium speed just until blended. Add eggs and vanilla extract and beat on medium speed until well blended, about 2 minutes. Stir in pecans just until blended. Spread batter evenly in pan.

Melt chocolate chips in a heavy 1- to 2-quart saucepan over low heat, stirring constantly. Add sweetened condensed milk and 1 tbs. butter and stir until well blended and butter has melted. Pour chocolate mixture in an even layer over batter in pan. Starting at one corner of pan, insert a table knife halfway down into batter and chocolate, but not to bottom of pan. Draw knife back and forth in a gentle, swirling motion from one side of pan to the other, down length of the pan, to create a marbled effect.

Bake in center of oven for 35 to 40 minutes or until a toothpick inserted in the center comes out clean, with a few moist crumbs, but not wet batter. Cool thoroughly in pan on a wire rack, about 1 hour.

Cut into 16 (2-by-3-inch) rectangular bars and remove from pan. Makes 16.

DEEP DARK CHOCOLATE-CHERRY CHEWS

You can find dried cherries in gourmet shops, health food stores and some large grocery stores. To make these chews even more sinful, serve them with cherry ice cream. You can also replace the dried cherries with finely chopped dried mango.

2 tsp. butter

1 tbs. unsweetened cocoa powder

1½ cups dried tart red cherries

2 cups Oreo® chocolate cookie crumbs, or 32 Famous™ Chocolate Wafers, ground into 2 cups fine crumbs with a food processor

2 tbs. unsweetened cocoa powder

2 large eggs

1 large egg white

¾ cup granulated sugar

2 tsp. pure vanilla extract

¼ tsp. salt

Heat oven to 350°F. Grease an 8-inch square baking pan with 2 tsp. butter. Dust with cocoa powder; invert pan and tap to release excess.

Toss cherries and chocolate cookie crumbs in 2 tbs. cocoa powder until evenly coated and set aside.

With an electric mixer, beat eggs, egg white, sugar, vanilla and salt on high speed in a large bowl for 2 minutes, or until mixture is pale and thickened. Remove bowl from mixer. Working quickly with a rubber spatula, gently fold in cherry-cookie crumb mixture just until combined and no white streaks are visible. (Do not overmix.) Spread batter evenly in pan.

Bake in center of oven for 30 to 35 minutes or until a toothpick inserted in the center comes out clean with a few moist crumbs, but not wet batter. Cool thoroughly in pan on a wire rack, about 1 hour.

Cut into 16 (2-inch) square bars and remove from pan. Makes 16.

DELUXE BLONDIES

These are quite delicious alone, or topped with chocolate frosting.

2 tsp. butter
1 tbs. unbleached all-purpose flour
¾ cup butterscotch chips
1 tbs. unbleached all-purpose flour
½ cup butter, melted and cooled
¾ cup butterscotch chips, melted and cooled (see page 6)
1 cup unbleached all-purpose flour
½ tsp. baking powder
¼ tsp. salt
¾ cup dark brown sugar, packed
¼ cup granulated sugar
1 large egg, lightly beaten
1 large egg yolk, lightly beaten
1 tsp. pure vanilla extract

Heat oven to 350°F. Grease an 8-inch square baking pan with 2 tsp. butter. Dust with 1 tbs. flour; invert pan and tap to release excess.

Stir melted butter and melted butterscotch chips together in a large bowl until well blended. Stir in flour, baking powder, salt, brown sugar and granulated sugar until well blended. Stir in egg, egg yolk and vanilla until well blended. Stir in flour-coated butterscotch chip mixture just until blended. Pour batter into pan.

Bake in center of oven for 30 to 40 minutes, or until a toothpick inserted in the center comes out clean with a few moist crumbs, but not wet batter. Cool thoroughly in pan on a wire rack, about 1 hour.

Cut into 16 (2-inch) square bars and remove from pan. Makes 16.

THREE-GINGER BROWNIES WITH SEMISWEET CHOCOLATE CHUNKS

Ground ginger, fresh ginger and crystallized ginger add plenty of sweet spice to these unusual brownies.

2 tsp. butter
1 tbs. unbleached all-purpose flour
2¼ cups unbleached all-purpose flour
2 tsp. ground ginger
2 tsp. baking soda
½ tsp. salt
¾ cup butter, softened
1 cup dark brown sugar, packed
½ cup dark molasses
1 large egg, lightly beaten
¼ cup grated peeled fresh ginger, packed
½ cup finely chopped crystallized ginger
6 oz. semisweet chocolate, cut into ½-inch chunks
2 tbs. unbleached all-purpose flour
⅛ cup confectioners' sugar

Heat oven to 350°F. Grease an 8-inch square baking pan with 2 tsp. butter. Dust with 1 tbs. flour; invert pan and tap to release excess.

Sift 2¼ cups flour, ground ginger, baking soda and salt onto a sheet of waxed paper. With an electric mixer, beat butter and brown sugar on medium speed until light and fluffy, about 2 minutes. Beat in molasses just until blended. Beat in dry ingredients on low speed just until blended. Beat in egg and grated ginger on medium speed just until mixture is well blended.

Toss crystallized ginger and chocolate chunks in 2 tbs. flour in a small bowl until evenly coated; set aside. Remove bowl from mixer and stir in the crystallized ginger-chocolate-flour mixture just until blended. Spread batter evenly in pan.

Bake in center of oven for 20 to 25 minutes, or until a toothpick inserted in the center comes out clean with a few moist crumbs, but not wet batter. (Note: The top may be uneven, but will level out as brownies cool.) Cool thoroughly in pan on a wire rack, about 1 hour.

Run a paring knife around inside edge of pan. Sift confectioners' sugar over top in an even layer. Cut into 16 (2-inch) square bars and remove from pan. Makes 16.

CHRISTMAS CRANBERRY-CHOCOLATE TEA SQUARES

They aren't brownies or blondies, but they are scrumptious! Try these tea squares for Christmas, or for any special occasion. Dried cranberries can be found in large supermarkets (Ocean Spray calls them "craisins," and some companies call them "crannies").

2 tsp. butter
1 tbs. unbleached all-purpose
   flour
1 cup butter, softened
$^1\!/_2$ cup confectioners' sugar
2 tsp. pure vanilla extract

2 cups unbleached all-purpose
   flour
$^1\!/_4$ tsp. baking powder
$^1\!/_4$ tsp. salt
1 cup dried cranberries
$^1\!/_2$ cup semisweet chocolate chips

TOPPING
1 can (16 oz.) whole berry cranberry sauce

Prepare tea squares: Heat oven to 350°F. Grease an 8-inch square baking pan with 2 tsp. butter. Dust with 1 tbs. flour; invert pan and tap to release excess.

With an electric mixer, beat butter, confectioners' sugar and vanilla on medium speed in a large bowl until light and creamy, about 2 minutes. Remove bowl from mixer. Sift flour, baking powder and salt onto a sheet of waxed paper. Add dry ingredients with dried cranberries and chocolate chips to bowl and stir gently with a rubber spatula to blend just until a soft dough forms, being careful not to overmix. With back of a large spoon, firmly press dough into pan in an even layer and smooth top.

Bake in center of oven for 5 minutes. Reduce oven temperature to 300°F and bake for 20 to 25 more minutes, or until a toothpick inserted in the center comes out clean with a few moist crumbs, but not wet batter, and edges are light golden brown. Cool thoroughly in pan on a wire rack, about 1 hour.

Run a paring knife around inside edge of pan. Spread whole berry cranberry sauce over tea squares in an even layer. Cut into 16 (2-inch) square bars and remove from pan. Makes 16.

OATMEAL APPLESAUCE BREAKFAST BLONDIES

These blondies are packed with walnuts and raisins and other good things to eat. They make a perfect start to a busy day.

TOPPING

1 cup old-fashioned oatmeal (not quick-cooking)
3/4 cup unbleached all-purpose flour

1 cup light brown sugar, packed
1 1/2 tsp. ground cinnamon
1/2 cup butter, melted

BLONDIES

2 tsp. butter
1 tbs. unbleached all-purpose flour
1/2 cup coarsely chopped walnuts
3/4 cup dark or golden raisins
2 tbs. unbleached all-purpose flour
1 1/4 cups unbleached all-purpose flour
1/2 tsp. baking powder
1/4 tsp. baking soda
1/4 tsp. salt

1/2 tsp. ground cinnamon
1/2 tsp. ground nutmeg
1/2 tsp. ground ginger
1/2 cup butter, melted and cooled
1/2 cup light brown sugar, packed
1/2 cup granulated sugar
2 large eggs, lightly beaten
1/2 tsp. pure vanilla extract
1/2 cup applesauce

Stir together topping ingredients in a medium bowl until well blended. Cover and refrigerate until ready to use.

Heat oven to 350°F. Grease an 8-inch square baking pan with 2 tsp. butter. Dust with 1 tbs. flour; invert pan and tap to release excess.

Combine walnuts, raisins and 2 tbs. flour in a small bowl until coated, and set aside.

Using a fork, vigorously stir together flour, baking powder, baking soda, salt, cinnamon, nutmeg and ginger in a medium bowl until well blended. Stir in melted butter, brown sugar, granulated sugar, eggs, vanilla and applesauce until well blended. Stir in walnut-raisin mixture until well blended. Spread batter evenly in pan.

Bake in center of oven for 10 minutes. Remove from oven and, working quickly, with your fingers break topping into dime-sized crumbs and sprinkle in an even layer over the top. Immediately return pan to oven and bake for 35 to 45 minutes, or until a toothpick inserted in the center comes out clean with a few moist crumbs, but not wet batter. Cool thoroughly in pan on a wire rack, about 1 hour.

Cut into 16 (2-inch) square bars and remove from pan. Makes 16.

PEACHES N' HONEY BARS

This is a very versatile recipe. Use whatever flavor pie filling pleases you most. Cherry or blueberry make a change.

2 tsp. butter
1 tbs. unbleached all-purpose flour
1/2 cup butter, softened
1/4 cup granulated sugar
1/2 cup honey
1 cup unbleached all-purpose flour
1/2 tsp. baking powder
1/4 tsp. baking soda
1 large egg, lightly beaten
1 can (21 oz.) peach pie filling

DRIZZLE
2 oz. semisweet chocolate
1/2 tsp. vegetable shortening

Heat oven to 350°F. Grease an 8-inch square baking pan with 2 tsp. butter. Dust with 1 tbs. flour; invert pan and tap to release excess.

With an electric mixer, beat softened butter and granulated sugar on medium speed until light and fluffy, about 2 minutes. Beat in honey just until blended. Beat in flour, baking powder and baking soda on low speed just until blended. Beat in egg on medium speed just until mixture is well blended. Spread batter evenly in pan.

Bake in center of oven for 20 to 25 minutes, or until a toothpick inserted in the center comes out clean with a few moist crumbs, but not wet batter, and the edges begin to pull away from sides of pan. Cool thoroughly in pan on a wire rack, about 1 hour.

Run a paring knife around inside edge of pan. Spread evenly with peach pie filling.

To prepare drizzle: Combine chocolate and shortening in a heavy 1-quart saucepan over low heat. Cook, stirring constantly, until mixture is melted and smooth. With a large spoon, pour in a thin, steady stream over bars in a decorative pattern. Let stand until drizzle is set, about 15 minutes, before serving.

Cut into 16 (2-inch) square bars and remove from pan. Makes 16.

THANKSGIVING PUMPKIN BLONDIES

Folks are always searching for a different dessert to add to the traditional fare on the groaning Thanksgiving board. These are good to serve if the celebration is at your home, or if you carry them to another.

CRUMBS

6 tbs. vegetable oil
1/3 cup dark molasses
1/2 cup light brown sugar, packed

1 1/2 cups unbleached all-purpose
  flour
1 tsp. ground cinnamon

BLONDIES

2 tsp. butter
1 tbs. unbleached all-purpose
  flour
1 1/4 cups unbleached all-purpose
  flour
1/4 tsp. baking powder
1/4 tsp. salt
3/4 tsp. ground ginger

1/2 cup light brown sugar, packed
1/4 cup granulated sugar
6 tbs. butter, melted and cooled
1 large egg, lightly beaten
1 tsp. pure vanilla extract
1 cup canned pumpkin, packed
3/4 cup milk chocolate chips

Prepare crumbs: In a medium bowl, combine crumb ingredients with your fingers until well blended; continue until a soft dough forms. Cover and set aside.

Prepare blondies: Heat oven to 350°F. Grease an 8-inch square baking pan with 2 tsp. butter. Dust with 1 tbs. flour; invert pan and tap to release excess.

With a fork, vigorously stir together 1¼ cups flour, baking powder, salt, ginger, brown sugar and granulated sugar in a medium bowl until well blended. Stir in melted butter, egg, vanilla extract and pumpkin until well blended and smooth. Stir in chocolate chips just until blended. Spread batter evenly in pan. With your fingers, break off quarter-sized pieces ("crumbs") of molasses mixture. Sprinkle evenly over top.

Bake in center of oven for 25 to 35 minutes, or until a toothpick inserted in the center comes out clean with a few moist crumbs, but not wet batter. Cool thoroughly in the pan on a wire rack, about 1 hour.

Cut into 8 (4-by-2-inch) rectangular bars and remove from pan. Makes 8.

BANANA BLONDIES WITH COCONUT CREAM

This dessert takes tropical flavor to delicious heights.

2 tsp. butter
1 tbs. unbleached all-purpose flour
1/4 cup butter, melted and cooled
3/4 cup mashed ripe bananas
   (about 2 medium-sized ripe
   bananas)
3/4 cup unbleached all-purpose
   flour

1/2 tsp. baking powder
1/4 tsp. salt
1/2 tsp. ground cinnamon
1/2 tsp. ground nutmeg
1/2 tsp. ground ginger
2/3 cup light brown sugar, packed
1 large egg, lightly beaten
3/4 tsp. banana extract

TOPPING

1 pkg. (5.1 oz.) vanilla-flavored Jell-O® Instant Pudding and Pie Filling,
   prepared according to package directions and chilled
1 tsp. banana extract
1 cup sweetened, flaked coconut, toasted and cooled (see page 11)

Heat oven to 350°F. Grease an 8-inch square baking pan with 2 tsp. butter. Dust with 1 tbs. flour; invert pan and tap to release excess.

With a fork, vigorously stir together melted butter and mashed banana in a large bowl until well blended. Stir in flour, baking powder, salt, cinnamon, nutmeg, ginger and brown sugar until well blended. Stir in lightly beaten egg and banana extract until well blended. Spread batter evenly in pan.

Prepare topping: Stir together prepared vanilla pudding, banana extract and toasted coconut in a medium bowl until well blended. Cover and refrigerate until set, about 2 hours.

Bake in center of oven for 25 to 35 minutes, or until a toothpick inserted in the center comes out clean with a few moist crumbs, but not wet batter. Cool thoroughly in pan on a wire rack, about 1 hour.

Run a paring knife around the inside edge of pan. With a metal spatula, gently loosen blondies and invert onto a serving plate. Just before serving, spread chilled topping evenly over blondies. Cut into 8 (4-x-2-inch) rectangular bars. Cover and store uneaten blondies on the serving plate in the refrigerator up to 1 week. Makes 8.

TWO-CHOCOLATE DRIED CHERRY BARS

The marriage of cherry and two chocolates is an amazing flavor combination. You can substitute finely chopped dried apricots or strawberries for the dried cherries.

2 tsp. butter
1 tbs. unbleached all-purpose flour
¾ cup dried tart red cherries
3 oz. white chocolate, coarsely chopped
3 oz. bittersweet chocolate, coarsely chopped
2 tbs. unbleached all-purpose flour
1⅛ cups unbleached all-purpose flour
¾ tsp. salt
⅔ cup granulated sugar
½ cup butter, melted and cooled
3 oz. white chocolate, melted and cooled (see page 5)
3 large eggs, lightly beaten
2 tsp. pure vanilla extract

Heat oven to 350°F. Grease an 8-inch square baking pan with 2 tsp. butter. Dust with 1 tbs. flour; invert pan and tap to release excess.

Toss dried cherries and chopped chocolates in 2 tbs. flour until coated; set aside.

Sift 1 1/8 cups flour, salt and sugar into a large bowl. Add melted butter and melted white chocolate, eggs and vanilla. Stir vigorously with a fork until well blended. Stir in flour-coated cherries and chocolate just until blended. Spread batter evenly in pan.

Bake in center of oven for 25 to 35 minutes or until a toothpick inserted in the center comes out clean, with a few moist crumbs, but not wet batter. Cool thoroughly in pan on a wire rack, about 1 hour.

Cut into 16 (2-inch) square bars and remove from pan. Makes 16.

SUNSHINE BARS WITH FUDGE ICING

The colors of summer inspire the title and the choice of oranges in several forms for the main flavor.

2 tsp. butter
1 tbs. unbleached all-purpose flour
1/2 cup butter, softened
1 cup confectioners' sugar
1/2 cup orange marmalade
2 tbs. frozen orange juice concentrate, thawed
1 tsp. orange extract or pure vanilla extract
1 1/2 cups unbleached all-purpose flour
1/2 tsp. baking powder
1/4 tsp. salt
1 large egg, lightly beaten

ICING
3 oz. semisweet chocolate
1/4 cup heavy whipping cream

Heat oven to 350°F. Grease an 8-inch square baking pan with 2 tsp. butter. Dust with 1 tbs. flour; invert pan and tap to release excess.

With an electric mixer, beat butter and confectioners' sugar on medium speed in a medium bowl until light and fluffy, about 2 minutes. Beat in marmalade, juice concentrate and orange extract until well blended, about 1 minute. Beat in flour, baking powder, salt and lightly beaten egg until well blended, about 1 minute. Spread batter evenly in pan.

Bake in center of oven for 20 to 25 minutes, or until a toothpick inserted in the center comes out clean with a few moist crumbs, but not wet batter, and tops of bars are lightly golden brown. Cool thoroughly in pan on a wire rack, about 1 hour.

Prepare icing: In a heavy 1-quart saucepan, melt chocolate over low heat, stirring constantly (see page 5). Add cream and cook for 30 seconds more, stirring constantly, until well blended and smooth. Remove from heat and let stand for 15 minutes to cool before using.

Run a paring knife around inside edge of pan. Pour icing over bars in an even layer, and let stand until firm, about 20 minutes. Cut into 16 (2-inch) square bars and remove with a metal spatula. Makes 16.

BUTTERSCOTCH-COCONUT BARS

The butterscotch chips can be replaced with peanut butter chips.

2 tsp. butter
1 tbs. unbleached all-purpose flour
3/4 cup butterscotch chips
2/3 cup sweetened, flaked coconut
2 tbs. unbleached all-purpose flour
1/2 cup butter, melted and cooled
3/4 cup butterscotch chips, melted and cooled (see page 6)
1 cup unbleached all-purpose flour
1/2 tsp. baking powder
1/4 tsp. salt
3/4 cup dark brown sugar, packed
1/4 cup granulated sugar
1 large egg, lightly beaten
1 large egg yolk, lightly beaten
1 tsp. pure vanilla extract

Heat oven to 350°F. Grease an 8-inch square baking pan with 2 tsp. butter. Dust with 1 tbs. flour; invert pan and tap to release excess. Toss ³/₄ cup butterscotch chips and flaked coconut in 2 tbs. flour to coat; set aside.

Stir melted butter and melted butterscotch chips together in a large bowl until well blended. Stir in flour, baking powder, salt, brown sugar and granulated sugar until well blended. Stir in egg, egg yolk and vanilla until well blended. Stir in the butterscotch chip-coconut mixture just until blended. Spread batter evenly in pan.

Bake in center of oven for 30 to 40 minutes, or until a toothpick inserted in the center comes out clean with a few moist crumbs, but not wet batter. Cool thoroughly in the pan on a wire rack, about 1 hour.

Cut into 16 (2-inch) square bars and remove from pan. Makes 16.

APRICOT-WHITE CHOCOLATE DREAMS
WITH ALPINE CURLS

This is truly a sophisticated white chocolate blondie, a must for the next party you host to "wow" your guests.

2 tsp. butter
1 tbs. unbleached all-purpose flour
6 oz. dried apricots, finely chopped
3 oz. white chocolate, coarsely chopped
2 tbs. unbleached all-purpose flour
1 1/8 cups unbleached all-purpose flour
3/4 tsp. salt
2/3 cup granulated sugar
1/2 cup butter, melted and cooled
3 oz. white chocolate, melted and cooled (see page 5)
3 large eggs, lightly beaten
2 tsp. pure vanilla extract
1/3 cup apricot preserves
1 bar (4 oz.) white chocolate, room temperature, for garnish

Heat oven to 350°F. Grease an 8-inch square baking pan with 2 tsp. butter. Dust with 1 tbs. flour; invert pan and tap to release excess.

Toss chopped apricots and white chocolate in 2 tbs. flour to coat; set aside.

Sift 1 1/8 cups flour, salt and sugar into a large bowl. Add melted butter and melted white chocolate, eggs and vanilla. Stir vigorously with a fork until well blended. Stir in apricot-white-chocolate mixture just until blended. Spread batter evenly in pan.

Bake in center of oven for 25 to 35 minutes or until surface is uniformly colored with no large indentations, and a toothpick inserted in the center comes out clean, with a few moist crumbs, but not wet batter. Cool thoroughly in the pan on a wire rack, about 1 hour.

Brush surface with apricot preserves. Cut into 16 (2-inch) square bars and remove from pan. With flat side of white chocolate bar facing up, draw a vegetable peeler across surface of chocolate. Scatter curls over blondies and serve. Store uneaten brownies in the refrigerator. Makes 16.

FROSTED PEANUT BUTTER LUNCHBOX BARS

For a quick garnish and a marbled effect, use a table knife to swirl raspberry preserves through the frosting after blondies have been frosted.

2 tsp. butter
1 tbs. unbleached all-purpose flour
1 cup unbleached all-purpose flour
1 tsp. baking powder
1/4 tsp. baking soda
1/4 tsp. salt
2/3 cup creamy peanut butter
1/4 cup butter, softened
1 cup light brown sugar, packed
2 large eggs, lightly beaten
1 tsp. pure vanilla extract

FROSTING
1 cup creamy-style peanut butter
1/4 cup confectioners' sugar, sifted

Heat oven to 350°F. Grease an 8-inch square baking pan with 2 tsp. butter. Dust with 1 tbs. flour; invert pan and tap to release excess.

Sift together 1 cup flour, baking powder, baking soda and salt onto a sheet of waxed paper and set aside. With an electric mixer, beat peanut butter, butter and brown sugar on medium speed in a large bowl until light and fluffy, about 2 minutes. Add eggs and vanilla and beat until well blended, about 1 minute. On low speed, beat in dry mixture for 30 seconds. Remove bowl from mixer and stir with rubber spatula until well blended and no white streaks are visible. Spread batter evenly in pan.

Bake in center of oven for 30 to 35 minutes, or until a toothpick inserted in the center comes out clean with a few moist crumbs, but not wet batter, and surface is dark golden brown. Cool thoroughly in pan on a wire rack, about 1 hour.

Combine frosting ingredients in a medium bowl with an electric mixer fitted with a paddle. Beat on low speed for 30 seconds. Then beat on high for 1 minute until mixture is thick and pale.

Run a paring knife around inside edge of pan and invert bars onto a serving plate. Evenly spread frosting over surface. Cut into 16 (2-inch) square bars. Makes 16.

WHITE CHOCOLATE MACADAMIA NUT BLONDIES

Macadamia nuts paired with white chocolate is true decadence. An equal amount of pistachio nuts is also inviting; purchase those with natural white shells, and shell and chop them yourself.

2 tsp. butter
1 tbs. unbleached all-purpose flour
1 cup white chocolate chips
4 oz. macadamia nuts, coarsely chopped
2 tbs. unbleached all-purpose flour
1 1/8 cups unbleached all-purpose flour
3/4 tsp. salt
2/3 cup granulated sugar
1/2 cup butter, melted and cooled
3 oz. white chocolate, melted and cooled (see page 5)
3 large eggs, lightly beaten
2 tsp. pure vanilla extract

Heat oven to 350°F. Grease an 8-inch square baking pan with 2 tsp. butter. Dust with 1 tbs. flour; invert pan and tap to release excess.

Toss white chocolate chips and chopped nuts in 2 tbs. flour to coat; set aside.

Sift 1 1/8 cups flour, salt and granulated sugar into a large bowl. Add melted butter, melted white chocolate, eggs and vanilla extract. Stir vigorously with a fork until mixture is well blended. Stir in chocolate-macadamia mixture just until blended. Spread batter evenly in pan.

Bake in center of oven for 25 to 35 minutes or until surface is uniformly colored with no large indentations, and a toothpick inserted in the center comes out clean, with a few moist crumbs, but not wet batter. Cool thoroughly in the pan on a wire rack, about 1 hour.

Cut into 16 (2-inch) square bars and remove from pan. Makes 16.

INDEX

A

Almond-cheesecake brownies 12
Altitude 3
Applesauce oatmeal breakfast
 blondies 52
Apricot-white chocolate dreams
 with alpine curls 66

B

Baking variations 9
Banana blondies with coconut
 cream 58
Blondies
 apricot-white chocolate dreams
  with alpine curls 66
 banana, with coconut cream
  58
 butterscotch-coconut bars 64
 deluxe 46

frosted peanut butter lunchbox
 bars 68
oatmeal applesauce breakfast
 52
peaches n' honey bars 54
sunshine bars with fudge icing
 62
Thanksgiving pumpkin 56
three-ginger with semisweet
 chocolate chunks 48
two-chocolate dried cherry
 bars 60
white chocolate macadamia
 nut 70
Breakfast blondies, oatmeal
 applesauce 52
Butter
 melted, about 3, 4
 softened 3
 unsalted 3
Butterscotch-coconut bars 64

C

Cake-like brownies
  cappuccino 24
  chocolate-sour cream frosted
    28
  with maple-pecan glaze 30
  mint meltaways 26
  ultimate double-chocolate 22
Cappuccino brownies 24
Caramel fudgy brownies 14
Cheesecake-almond brownies 12
Cheesecake frosted brownies 40
Cherry, dried, and two-chocolate
    bars 60
Cherry, deep dark chocolate
    chews 44
Chewy brownies
  with cheesecake frosting 40
  chocolate piña colada 34
  deep dark chocolate-cherry
    chews 44
  lemon bars with black bottom
    crust 38

macaroon 36
  sensationally 32
  two-toned milk chocolate-
    pecan 42
Chocolate
  -cranberry Christmas tea
    squares 50
  deep dark cherry chews 44
  double, ultimate brownies 22
  melting, about 3
  milk, and pecan two-toned
    brownies 42
  -piña colada brownies 34
  semisweet chunks in three-
    ginger brownies 48
  -sour cream frosted brownies
    28
  two, and dried cherry bars 60
Christmas cranberry-chocolate tea
    squares 50
Coconut-butterscotch bars 64
Coconut cream in banana
    blondies 58

Coconut, how to toast
Cutting, about 6

D

Deluxe blondies 46

F

Fudgy brownies
almond-cheesecake 12
caramel 14
marbled 18
raspberry truffle 20
rocky roads 16
supreme 10

H

Honey n' peaches bars 54

I

Ingredients
about 3-5
measurements 2, 3
temperature 3

L

Lemon bars with black bottom
crust 38
Lunchbox bars, frosted peanut
butter 68

M

Macadamia nut white chocolate
blondies 70
Macaroon brownies, chewy 36
Maple-pecan glazed brownies 30
Marbled brownies 18
Mint meltaways 26
Mixing, about 5
Morsels, melting, about 4

N

Nuts, how to toast 9

O

Oatmeal applesauce breakfast blondies 52
Oven
    about 5, 6
    rack 5
    temperature 5, 6

P

Pans
    about 1, 2
    flouring 2
    greasing 2
    sizes 1
    surface 2
Peach n' honey bars 54
Peanut butter lunchbox bars, frosted 68

Pecan-maple glazed brownies 30
Pecan-milk chocolate two-toned brownies 42
Piña colada chocolate brownies 34
Pumpkin blondies, Thanksgiving 56

R

Raspberry truffle brownies 20
Rocky roads brownies 16

S

Sensationally chewy brownies 32
Serving variations 7-9
Sour cream-chocolate frosted brownies 28
Storage 6, 7
Sunshine bars with fudge icing 62
Supreme fudgy brownies 10

T

Tea squares, Christmas cranberry-chocolate 52

Thanksgiving pumpkin blondies 56

Three-ginger brownies with semi-sweet chocolate chunks 48

Truffle raspberry brownies 20

U

Ultimate double-chocolate brownies 22

W

White chocolate-apricot dreams with alpine curls 66

White chocolate macadamia nut blondies 70